LOUISE TALMA

SIX ETUDES

for Piano

ED-2464

ISBN 978-0-7935-1165-5

G. SCHIRMER, Inc.

DISTRIBUTED BY

HAL•LEONARD®
CORPORATION
7777 W. BLUEMOUND RD. P.O. BOX 13819 MILWAUKEE, WI 53213

www.musicsalesclassical.com
www.halleonard.com

Six Etudes

To Thornton Wilder

I

Louise Talma

45014

New York City
Dec. 2, 1953–Jan. 2, 1954

2:25

II

Prestissimo ♩=208

p sempre staccato, molto secco

sempre senza ped.

f very energetic, sempre cresc.

ff *p sempre staccato*

cresc.

mf *cresc.* *f* *cresc.*

sff *f* *mf* *f* *sff*

45014

1: 21

New York City
Sept. 24, - Nov. 16, 1953

To John Edmunds

III

For the study of the sostenuto pedal

The sostenuto pedal *only* is to be used throughout this piece for the exact duration of the sustained tones. The damper pedal is not to be used at all except in the one place where it is indicated (measures **25-27**).

45014

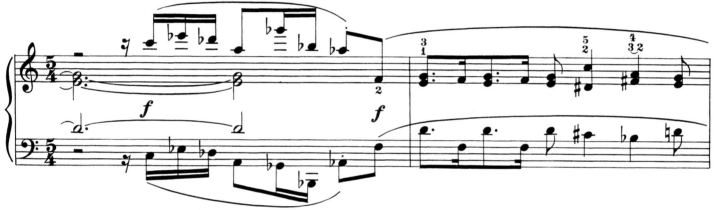

1:35

New York City
June 12-26, 1954

To Paul Nordoff

IV

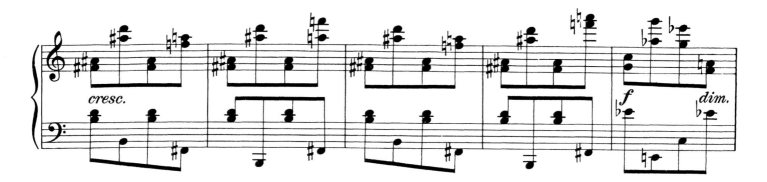

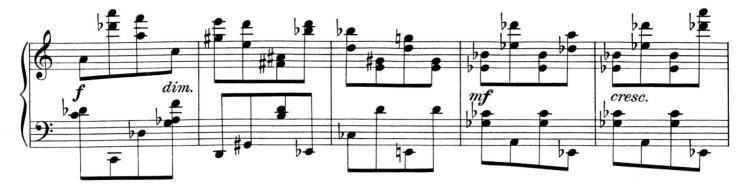

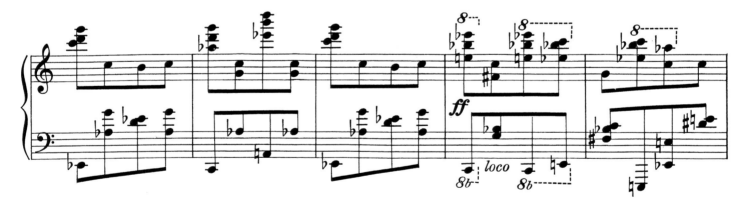

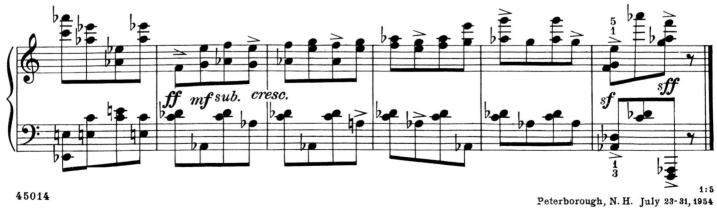

Peterborough, N. H. July 23-31, 1954

1:5

V

Allegretto grazioso ♪ = 176

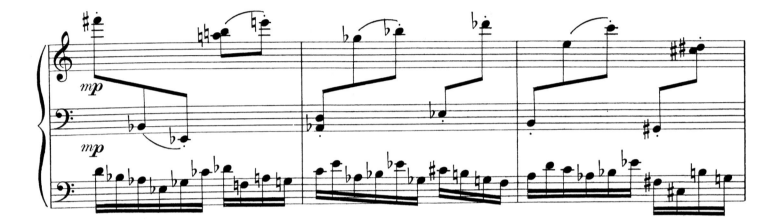

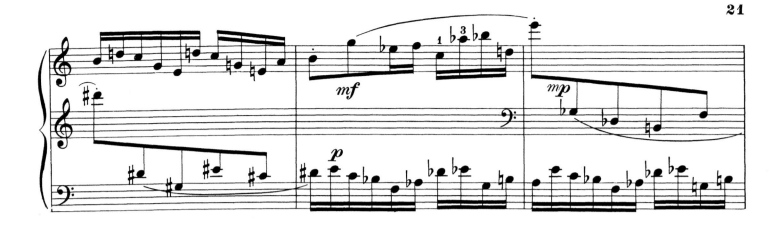

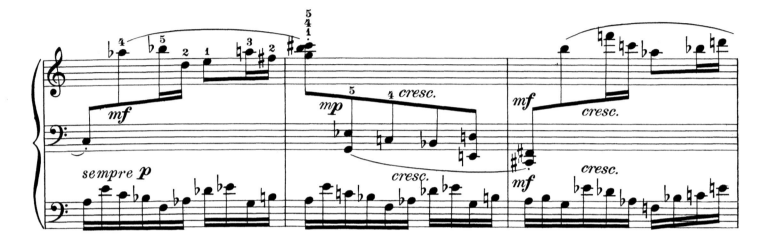

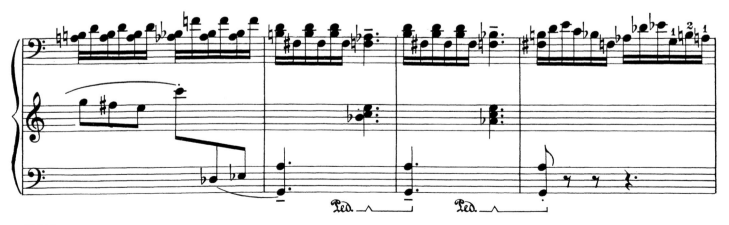

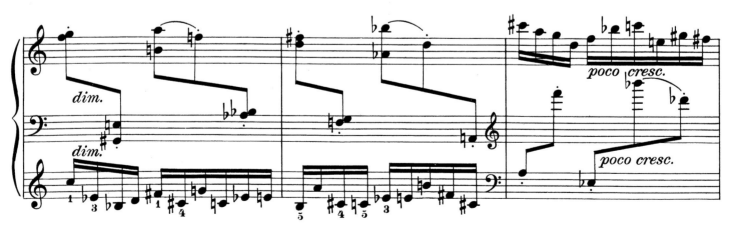

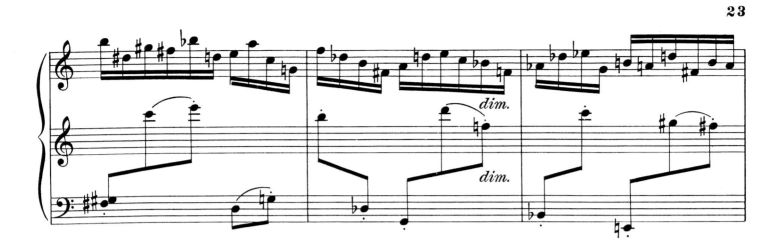

1:50

Peterborough, N. H. July 3-9, 1954.

To Beveridge Webster

VI

Molto adagio

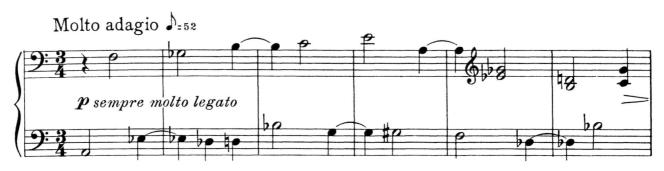

Except where it is marked the pedal is to be used in such a way as not to blur the passage work.

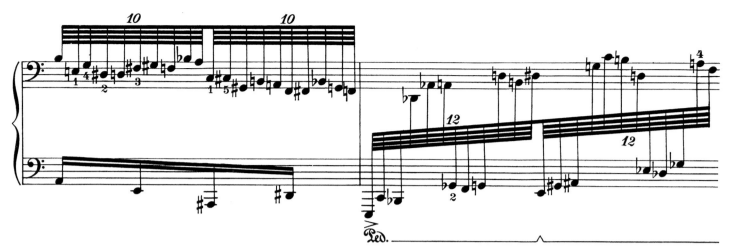

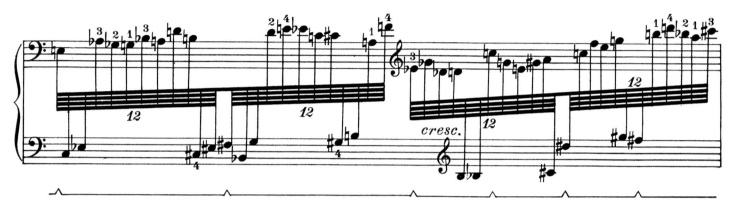

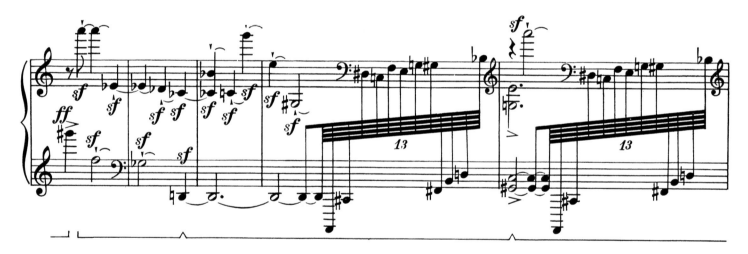

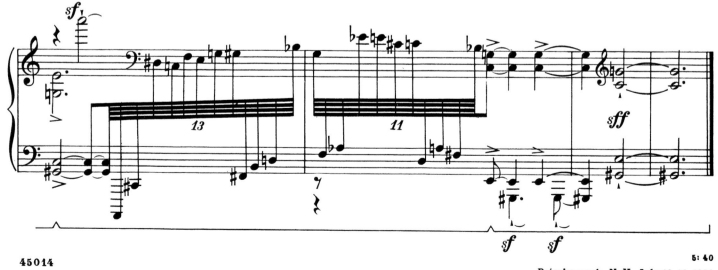

45014

5: 40

Peterborough, N. H. July 12-21, 1954